Chatterbox

ENGLISH AS A SECOND LANGUAGE

Centre de ressources de la Faculté d'éducation
Université d'Ottawa - University of Ottawa
Faculty of Education Resource Centre

Gillian Baxter
Hélène Bibeau

With contributions from Natalie Maltais

General Editor: Jonathan Munro Jones

Language-Acquisition Consultant: Patsy M. Lightbown, PhD

THIRD CYCLE, ELEMENTARY

STUDENT'S BOOK 1

ÉDITIONS DU RENOUVEAU PÉDAGOGIQUE INC.

5757, RUE CYPIHOT
SAINT-LAURENT (QUÉBEC)
H4S 1R3

TÉLÉPHONE : (514) 334-2690
TÉLÉCOPIEUR : (514) 334-4720
COURRIEL : erpidlm@erpi.com

Project editor
Jocelyne Lauzière

Cover and book design
Tandem Conception et Infographie inc.

Illustrations
Éric Allard: page 83; Chantale Audet: pages 83-90, 93-97; Danielle Bélanger: pages 1-11, 13-18, 20, 25-54, 57-60, 62-65, 71-73, 75-82, 91, 92, 98-103, 105-112, 121-135; Diane Blais: pages 21-24; Anne-Marie Charest: pages 66-70; Dave Garneau: pages 41-54, 103-112; Josée Masse: pages 113, 115-120; François Thisdale: pages 12, 74, 104, 114

Photo research and permissions
Pierre Richard Bernier

Photographs
Canadian Press Picture Archives, p. 56 (Loch Ness monster, Bigfoot), p. 61 (Godzilla)
Cath Wadforth/Science Photo Library/Publiphoto, p. 107 (flea)
Photo Gary Ombler/Dorling Kindersley Picture Library, p. 61 (velociraptor)
Shooting Star/Ponopresse, p. 61 (Ghidrah, King Kong)
Topham/Ponopresse, p. 56 (yeti)

In memory of my grandmother, Annie, with love. G.B.
To my parents, Jules and Edmée, with love. H.B.

Dépôt légal : 1ᵉ trimestre 2003
Bibliothèque nationale du Québec
National Library of Canada
Imprimé au Canada

ISBN 2-7613-1342-9
 234567890 IE   9876543
10533 ABCD   JS12

Contents

Strategies for Learning English 1

1 **That Looks Familiar!** 3

2 **Secrets from the Tomb** 11

3 **Every Drop Counts** 19

4 **Sweet Tooth** 31

5 **The Night of Giving** 41

6 **Monsters: Real or Fake?** 55

7   Tall Tales 65

8   The Case of the Stolen Guitar 73

9   Loonies and Toonies 83

10   Treasure Hunters 91

11   Don't Bug Me! 103

12   Up, Up and Away! 113

Project 1: Reader's Theatre 121

Project 2: You're On! 125

Chatterboxes 127

Strategies
for Learning English

Look it up.

Take risks.

Work with your classmates.

Pay attention.

Guess the meaning.

Don't worry if you don't understand everything.

Practise.

Find the important words.

Get ready to read
or to listen.

Check and correct
your work.

Take notes.

Plan your work.

Think about what
you already know.

Find the general
meaning.

When you don't know
the word for something,
describe it.

After each activity, ask
yourself these questions.

That Looks Familiar!

► **What do you remember from your English class last year?**

 **Make a learner's logbook.**

Warm-up

► **Name all the objects in the picture.**

Our English Class

Activity 1 | This Is Me

► **Complete the identification form.**

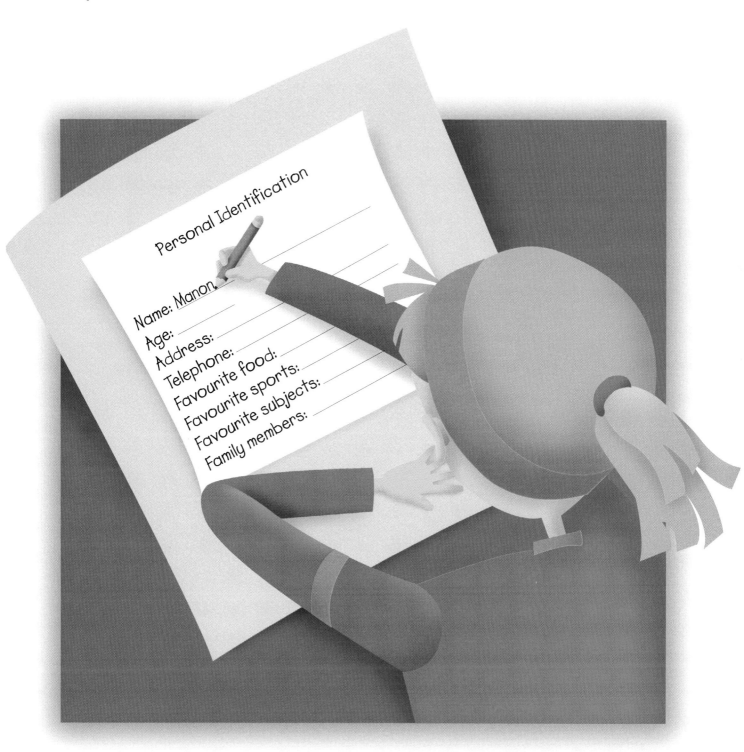

Personal Identification

Name: Manon
Age:
Address:
Telephone:
Favourite food:
Favourite sports:
Favourite subjects:
Family members:

Activity 2 · I Know That Word!

► Make a list of ten English words you know.
► Illustrate the words.

Activity 3 — Is That English?

▶ **Read the text.**
▶ **Identify four different types of English words.**

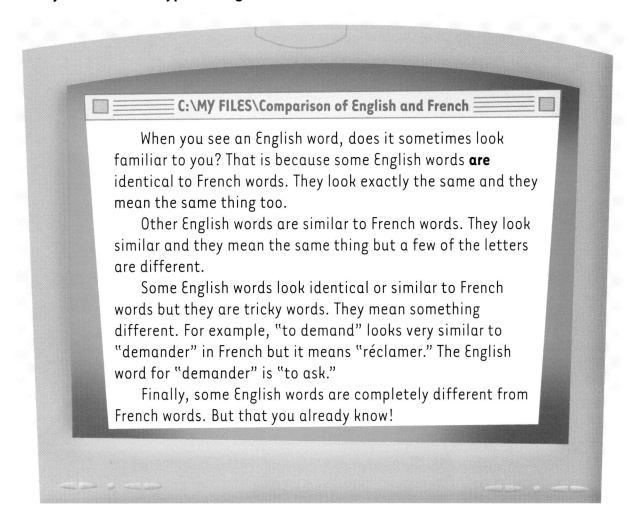

C:\MY FILES\Comparison of English and French

When you see an English word, does it sometimes look familiar to you? That is because some English words **are** identical to French words. They look exactly the same and they mean the same thing too.

Other English words are similar to French words. They look similar and they mean the same thing but a few of the letters are different.

Some English words look identical or similar to French words but they are tricky words. They mean something different. For example, "to demand" looks very similar to "demander" in French but it means "réclamer." The English word for "demander" is "to ask."

Finally, some English words are completely different from French words. But that you already know!

▶ **Look at the pages in this unit.**
▶ **Find eight words that are identical or similar to French words.**

That Looks Familiar!

Activity 4 English All around Me

► Find English words around you.

Make a learner's logbook.

▶ **Decorate the front cover of your logbook.**

Learner's Logbook for English

▶ **Glue your identification form onto the inside of the front cover.**

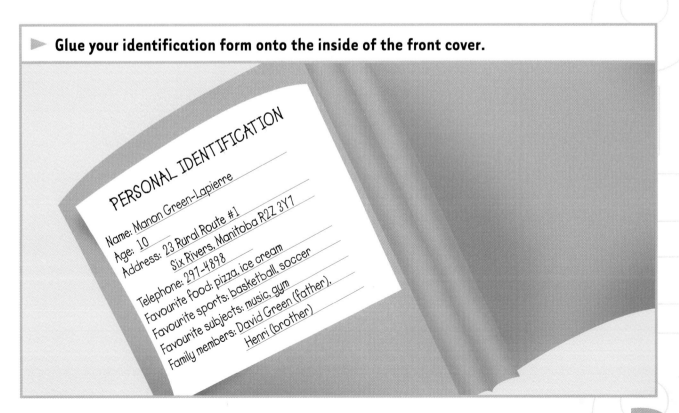

PERSONAL IDENTIFICATION

Name: Manon Green-Lapierre
Age: 10
Address: 23 Rural Route #1
Six Rivers, Manitoba R2Z 3Y7
Telephone: 297-4898
Favourite food: pizza, ice cream
Favourite sports: basketball, soccer
Favourite subjects: music, gym
Family members: David Green (father),
Henri (brother)

► **Glue your handout from activity 3 onto the inside of the back cover.**

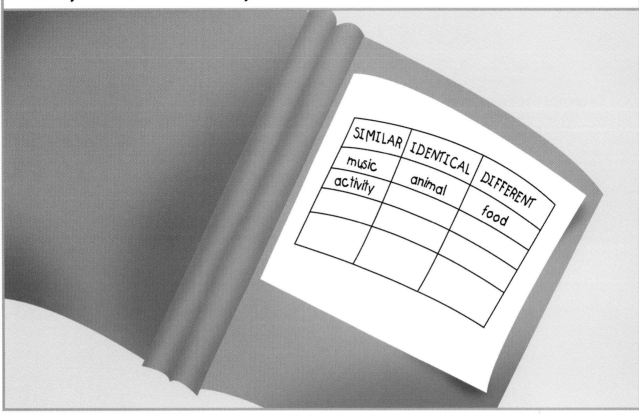

► **Write as many English words as you can on the back cover.**
► **Illustrate the words if you want.**

Unit 2

Secrets from the Tomb

► **Who is this boy?**
► **Why is he famous?**

 **Make a pyramid book.**

Warm-up

Chatterbox 4

▶ Complete the handout with words about Ancient Egypt.

Activity 1   Into the Tomb

▶ **Read the newspaper clipping.**

NOVEMBER 27, 1922

An amazing discovery!

Yesterday was a sensational day for Egypt and all the world! Howard Carter, a British archaeologist, discovered the tomb of Tutankhamen, the boy king. The nine-year-old boy became pharaoh in 1333 B.C. He died at the age of 18.

▶ **Listen to Carter's reports.**
▶ **Place the objects on the diagram.**

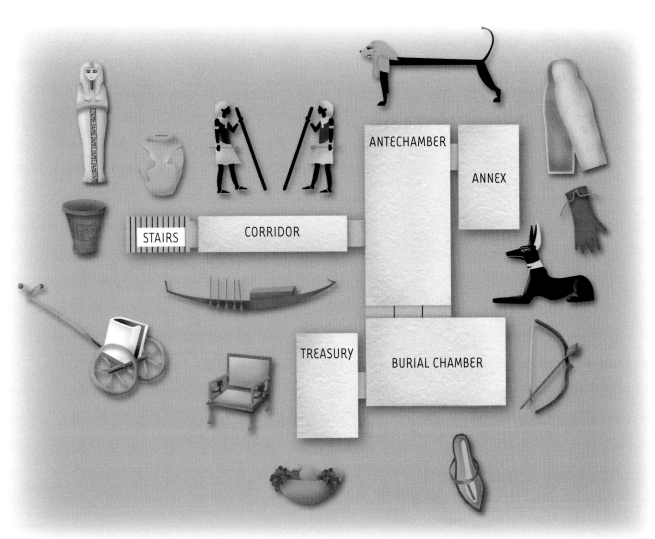

STAIRS   CORRIDOR   ANTECHAMBER   ANNEX   TREASURY   BURIAL CHAMBER

Activity 2 This Is My Life

▶ Choose objects for your pyramid.
▶ Tell your partner what they are.

I would put a telescope. I would have a skateboard.

I would put a book. I would have a hockey stick.

Activity 3 Ruler for a Day

► **Read a pharaoh's diary.**

I am Hatshepsut and I am pharaoh. I am 13 years old. I am a girl but I wear a man's clothes. I wear the clothes of a king. I am the king.

I am the king!!

I have many responsibilities. I must keep my people safe. I do not like war.

I want my people to live in a good and beautiful place. I love pretty things.

My people must have everything they need. My workers bring perfumes, spices, ivory and gold from distant lands.

Some people do not like me. They do not want me to be king. I will still do my best for my kingdom. I will make my people happy.

To do

1. Keep my kingdom at peace.
2. Keep my country clean.
3. Give my people the things they need.

The rules of my kingdom
(to be announced tomorrow morning)

1. You must not fight. (My people have to respect each other.)
2. You must not damage public property. (My people have to respect the environment.)
3. You must share with others. (My people have to help each other.)

► **Write the rules for your classroom.**

You **must** do your best.
You **have to** respect others.

Activity 4 — Written in Stone

▶ **Read the text.**

> Ancient Egyptians wrote in hieroglyphics. Hieroglyphics used symbols not letters. There were over 700 different signs. It was very difficult to learn.
>
> In 1799, French soldiers found a large black stone near Rosetta, Egypt. The Rosetta Stone was the key to understanding hieroglyphics.
>
> Jean Champollion was one of the first people to decode the Rosetta Stone's hieroglyphics.

▶ **Work with your teammates.**
▶ **Decode the hieroglyphics to find the words.**

T u t a n k h a m e n

1

5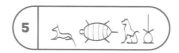

2

6

3

7

4

Wrap-up

Make a pyramid book.

▶ Make a pyramid book about yourself.

1. On the cover, write your name in hieroglyphics.

2. Inside, write a short text about yourself.

I am ten years old.

3. Write three things that you must do to be a good student.

I must respect my classmates.

4. Decorate the book with pictures that represent you.

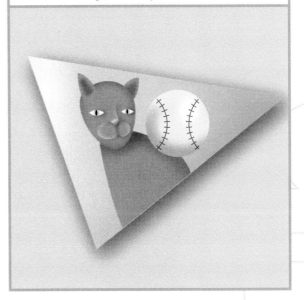

Word Box

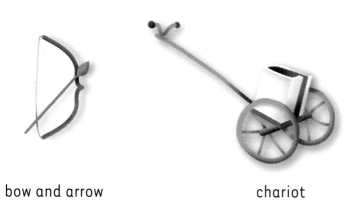

bow and arrow

chariot

coffin

couch

glove

gold

jar

mummy

sarcophagus

scroll

spices

Every Drop Counts

► **Is water important to you?**
► **Can we drink all the water around us?**

 Prepare a skit about water conservation.

Warm-up

► Identify how we use water.

Activity 1

How the Fly Saved the River

▶ **Read the story.**

An Ojibway Legend

Many, many years ago, there was a beautiful river. Its water was pure and sweet. Many fish and animals lived in the river and many animals came to the river to drink. All the animals and the fish loved the river and its sweet pure water.

One day a giant moose came to the river. He came to drink.
He was a huge moose and he was very, very thirsty.
He drank and he drank and he drank. Soon the
water started to sink lower and lower.
The more he drank, the lower
the water sank.

The beavers were worried.
The water was disappearing from around their lodges.
"Our homes will be destroyed," they said.

The deer and the foxes were worried.
"What will we drink if the water
disappears?" they asked.

The fish were worried. The water they lived in was disappearing. "Our homes will be destroyed," they said, "and we cannot live on the land."

All the animals and the fish wanted the moose to leave but he was so big and so strong that they were afraid of him.

"I will make the moose leave," said a little black fly. All the animals laughed. "A tiny fly cannot move a giant moose."

The fly said nothing. She just went to work. First she landed on the moose's leg and bit him. Then she landed on the moose's ear and bit him again. The moose shook himself and stamped his foot very hard on the ground. The fly landed on the moose's back. She landed on his head. She bit him again and again. The moose ran and jumped but the fly would not stop. Soon the moose ran away from the pesky fly and the river. He never came back again.

The animals were very grateful. Their river was safe. "Thank you. Thank you," they said to the fly.

The fly was very proud. "Even the very small can defeat the very strong if they use their brain to think," she said.

Activity 2 — How Much Water Do You Use?

▶ **Identify the area that uses the most water.**

Water consumption in a family home

Using water outdoors may double your water consumption.

Outdoors
Wash the car (400 L)
Clean
the driveway (250 L)
Water the lawn and garden for 30 minutes
(1050 L)

Bathroom
Flush the toilet (20 L)
Take a shower (100 L)
Take a bath (150 L)
Brush teeth (10 L)

Laundry room
Wash the clothes
(225 L)
Clean the house
(75 L)

Kitchen
Wash the dishes
by hand (35 L)
Use the dishwasher (40 L)
Cook (20 L)

► **Look at the amounts of water used in a typical family home.**
► **Estimate how much water you use in your house every week.**

 once a day, **twice** a day, **three times** a day

	Monday	Tuesday	Wednesday
once a day	X	X	X
twice a day	XX	XX	XX
three times a day	XXX	XXX	XXX

Activity 3 Save It, Don't Waste It

Chatterbox 11

▶ **Read the tips.**

▶ **Match each tip with the right picture.**

Use a bucket instead of a hose.

Turn off the tap. Don't let the water run.

A toilet is not a garbage can.

Fill up the dishwasher before using it.

1 Save every drop.

2 Help a river.

3 Leave water for the fish.

4 Stop wasting water.

▶ **Compare the water consumption of two people.**

Sally Saver

Wally Waster

Activity 4 Drip, Drip, Drip

▶ **Read the water-saving ads.**
▶ **Identify what you can do to save water.**

Don't let the drain drink all your water.

Use water-saving shower heads and faucet aerators.

Save water: fix the drip.

Fix all tap and toilet leaks.

Don't water the sidewalk.

Use a soaker hose.

Fill it up naturally.

Use a rain barrel.

▶ **Listen to the radio ads.**
▶ **Find out how much water you can save.**

Wrap-up

Prepare a skit about water conservation.

▶ **Present a situation that wastes water.**

▶ **Explain how much water is used.**

35 L
per minute

▶ **Suggest one solution to the problem.**

▶ **Invent a water-saving slogan.**

Fill it up naturally!

Word Box

bucket

household

shower head

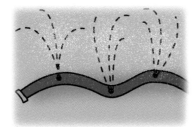

soaker hose

steam

DEFINITIONS

conservation:	protection of the natural environment
pesky:	irritating
(to) save:	to preserve
(to) waste:	to use more than is necessary

NUMBERS

20	twenty	60	sixty	100	one hundred
30	thirty	70	seventy	1000	one thousand
40	forty	80	eighty		
50	fifty	90	ninety		

GRAMMAR SECTION

Imperative verbs

Imperative verbs are used to give commands.

Affirmative commands

Use the main form of the verb.

Save the fish.

Fix your tap.

Negative commands

Use don't + the main form of the verb.

Don't waste water.

Don't wash your driveway.

Sweet Tooth

► **Do you like any of these treats?**
► **Which do you prefer?**

 **Invent a special treat.**

Warm-up

▶ Identify the treats we can make with chocolate.
▶ Identify the different ways we can eat ice cream.

Activity 1 Everybody Likes a Treat

Chatterbox 11

► Find out what treats your classmates like.

Question	Answer	Student's name
1. What's your favourite ice cream?		
2. What's your favourite chocolate bar?		

Activity 2 Did You Know?

► Listen to the text.
► Find out about chocolate.

► **Read the article.**
► **Now find out about ice cream.**

You scream, I scream, we all scream for ice cream

It is a very hot day in the summer. What is the first thing that you think of? Ice cream, of course! It can be vanilla, strawberry, chocolate or butterscotch. It doesn't matter. It's cold, it's refreshing and it's so-o-o good!

What is ice cream? Just frozen cream? No! Ice cream is made of cream, milk and sugar. It also contains one very important invisible ingredient: air! Ice-cream makers beat air into

the milk mixture when the mixture begins to freeze. This makes the ice cream light. Now you can take a big spoon and fill up your bowl.

Ice cream without air is not soft. Ice cream without air is just a block as hard as an iceberg. Imagine . . . It's 32 °C. You're hot. Your body is screaming for ice cream NOW. You run to the freezer. But what do you get? Just a broken spoon and an empty bowl!

Daily News

page B-12

Chocolate Dreams

Sweet Tooth

Activity 3 Going Bananas

▶ Read the recipes.
▶ Match each recipe with an illustration.

Banana Pizza

- Spread some chocolate sauce on a tortilla or a large cookie.
- Decorate the tortilla or cookie with slices of banana and other fruit.

Banana Surprise

- Peel and slice two bananas.
- Put the slices into a large bowl.
- Pour chocolate sauce over the bananas.
- Add chocolate ice cream.
- Add another layer of sliced bananas and oranges.
- Cover it all with whipped cream.

Banana Freeze

- Peel a banana and cut it in two.
- Insert a popsicle stick into the cut end.
- Dip each banana popsicle into some chocolate sauce.
- Dip each banana popsicle into candy sprinkles.
- Freeze the banana popsicle for two hours.

Banana Cookie Supreme

- Cut a banana into very small pieces.
- Put the pieces into a bowl.
- Break two chocolate chip cookies into very small pieces.
- Mix the banana pieces with the chocolate chip cookies.
- Sprinkle the mixture over vanilla ice cream.

Sweet Tooth

► **Look at the desserts.**
► **Tell your partner how you think each dessert tastes.**

Sweet: Sugar is sweet.
Crunchy: Peanuts are crunchy.
Smooth: Plain yogurt is smooth.

Wrap-up

Invent a special treat.

► **Decide what to put in your treat.**

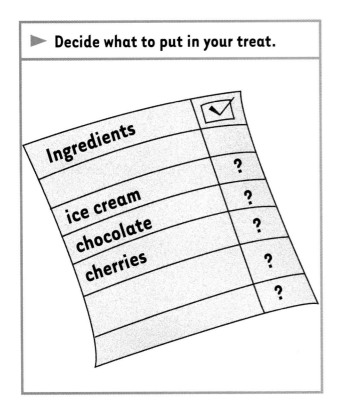

Ingredients	✓
	?
ice cream	?
chocolate	?
cherries	?
	?

► **Name your treat.**

~~Merry Cherry~~
Cherry Heaven

► **Describe your treat.**

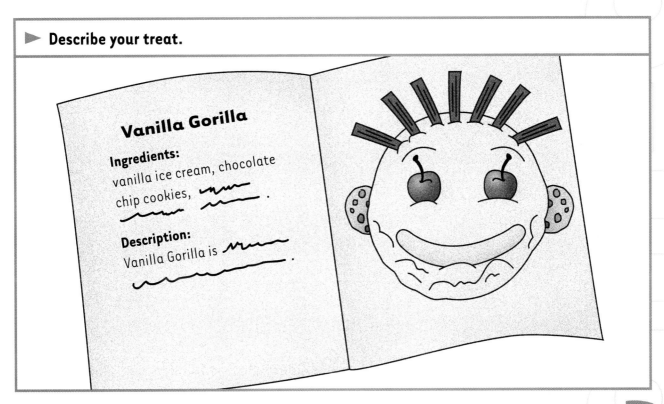

Vanilla Gorilla

Ingredients:
vanilla ice cream, chocolate chip cookies, ____ .

Description:
Vanilla Gorilla is ____ .

Word Box

cherry

cocoa bean

coconut

(to) dip

layer

marshmallow

milkshake

(to) peel

(to) pour

(to) slice

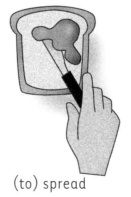
(to) spread

(to) sprinkle

Unit 4

The Night of Giving

► Can you name the celebrations seen in the picture?
► What can you give to others?

 Make a giving bag.

Warm-up

► **Look at the covers of the book.**

► **Complete the first two sentences on your bookmark.**

The Children of Kelm

J. M. Jones

The Night of Giving was a special time for all the children of Kelm. Then one night, something strange happened. Follow the children of Kelm on their journey to a new discovery. Will the children break the spell? Find out what happened when the children of Kelm learned to share.

"This book shows what can happen when people think about others."
— Books for Children Monthly

"A celebration of giving!"
— Kids' Book Review

ABC Children's Books Ltd.

Activity 1 The Children of Kelm

► Read the first part of the story.

A long time ago, in the beautiful village of Kelm, people celebrated the Night of Giving. On that night, they decorated the village with bright lights. The children of Kelm dressed in costumes of all kinds. They went from door to door. The adults answered the door and gave the children candy. Then the children sang a short song of thanks.

One Night of Giving, three children of Kelm—Muron, Shan and El—saw a stranger going from door to door. The stranger was wearing a costume but he was not a child of Kelm. Who was he? What was he doing here?

The three children quickly forgot about the stranger and went out to celebrate the Night of Giving. Soon the children noticed that the adults were not answering the door. The children were angry. They wanted their candy. The adults were not respecting the Night of Giving. Then, when the children went home, what did they find? Empty houses. Their parents were gone. There were no adults anywhere in Kelm.

▶ **On your story map, write information about the characters.**

	The characters are the people in the story.	*who*

Activity 2 A Year of Sadness

► **Read the next part of the story.**

At first the children thought their parents were playing a joke. By morning, they knew it was no joke.

What had happened to their parents? Where did they go? Why did they leave? Was it because the children didn't pick up their toys? Was it because they didn't eat their vegetables? Was it because they made a lot of noise?

"No," said Muron, who was very clever. "It was that stranger! **He** stole our parents! **He** put a spell on them!"

All the children agreed. They decided to find the stranger. It was not easy. There were no parents to help. There were no parents to make phone calls, no parents to drive them around, no parents to look up information. Days went by, weeks went by. Almost a whole year went by.

Every day the village of Kelm looked a little dirtier and a little sadder. Things were broken but there were no parents to fix them. Things were lost but there were no parents to find them. The children got tired of eating peanut butter sandwiches and drinking soda, but there were no parents to cook meals.

The children of Kelm missed their parents. They missed being kissed goodnight. Most of all, the children missed being hugged. Even Shan, who never let anyone hug him, missed it.

▶ **On your story map, write about the children's problems.**

 The storyline **is all the important events.** | ***events***

The Night of Giving

Activity 3 A New Discovery

► **Read the third part of the story.**

Finally, the children discovered where the mysterious stranger lived. He lived in a village across the valley. People said that it was a dirty and unhappy place. It had grey houses and brown grass and dark streets. There were no flowers and no places to play. It was called Sansson-de-Rire.

The children had to go to the village to find their parents but they were frightened. Muron had a plan. "We will go on the Night of Giving," he said. "People are kind then."

And so they went. When they entered Sansson-de-Rire, they were surprised. The village wasn't dirty and unhappy. The houses were decorated for the Night of Giving. The children smelled pumpkin pies, and pine logs burning in the fireplaces. Every house had flowers in the garden. There was a beautiful park with swings and slides. Everything was clean and bright.

The children knocked at the door of the first house. The door opened and there was Muron's mother.

"Mom!" cried Muron.

She laughed. "Very funny. Here you are, little boy." She gave him some candy and then she closed the door.

"She didn't know me," said Muron. "What's going on?"

"I can tell you." A little woman stood near them. She wore a long purple robe and a tall black hat with green stars and red moons on it.

▶ **Complete your story map with information about the setting.**
▶ **Complete the next section of your bookmark.**
▶ **Tell a partner what you think is going to happen.**

 The setting is where and when the story takes place. | **_where_ and _when_**

Activity 4 Thank You for Giving

▶ **Read the ending of the story.**

The children of Kelm gathered around the old woman. No one was afraid. She looked like a kind grandmother.

"All the adults of Sansson-de-Rire left," she said. "They were hypnotized by the Wicked Wizard of Makingmore. He forced them to work for him. Then he put a spell on your parents too. He made them come here to look after the children of Sansson-de-Rire."

The children were very quiet. Then Shan said, "That's very sad but we want our parents back."

"Wait a minute," said El, the small girl from Kelm, who had bright red hair. "It's the Night of Giving. It's the night of sharing. Why don't we share with the children of Sansson-de-Rire? We know how sad it is without parents. We can all live together."

The children began to nod. Yes. Yes. Yes. Every time a child nodded, a door opened. Parents came out and greeted their children from Kelm. They introduced them to their children from Sansson-de-Rire. The spell was broken. The parents and **all** their children stood in the village park. They sang the Night of Giving song.

The Night of Giving

"Thank you for opening your door. Thank you for sharing. Thank you for this night and thank you all for giving."

And so, because the children of Kelm cared enough to share, all the children and all the parents lived together, happily ever after.

▶ **Write the theme of the story on your story map.**
▶ **Complete the last two sentences on your bookmark.**

| **The theme is the main idea of the story.** | *message* |

Make a giving bag.

▶ Decorate your bag with pictures that represent giving.

▶ Choose four people that you want to give something to.

▶ Make a gift certificate for each person.

Remember! The best gifts are the ones that don't cost anything.

Word Box

broken

costume

hug

kind

kiss

nod

pine log

pumpkin pie

spell

stranger

wizard

GRAMMAR SECTION

Future tense   will + main verb   will not + main verb

be + going to + main verb   be + not going to + main verb

I will clean my room. I will share my things with my sister.
I will not fight with my brother.
I am going to clean my room. I am going to share my things with my sister.
I am not going to fight with my brother.

Unit 6

Monsters: Real or Fake?

- ► **Do you know these legendary creatures?**
- ► **Do you believe they exist?**

 **Create your own movie monster.**

Warm-up

► **Look at the pictures.**
► **Say whether you think they are real or fake.**

Footprint of the yeti, Nepal, 1951.

1

Loch Ness monster, Scotland, 1951.

2

3

Plaster cast of Bigfoot's foot, California, 1958

4

Loch Ness monster, Scotland, 1934.

5

Bigfoot, California, 1967.

Activity 1

Where Are They Hiding?

► **Read the following texts.**
► **Identify the places and the creatures.**

Lake Monsters

People have believed for centuries that monsters inhabit large, deep, cold lakes. Loch Ness, a lake in Scotland, is the home of a legendary creature called Nessie. In Canada, British Columbia's Okanagan Lake is well known for its monster, Ogopogo. Closer to home, Lake Memphrémagog in Québec is supposed to hide a monster called Memphré.

Sea Monsters

Long ago sailors believed that monsters hid at the bottom of the Atlantic and Pacific Oceans. They reported many encounters with creatures that resembled long snakes. They called them "sea serpents." Reports of attacks by the "kraken," another legendary sea monster, scared many Scandinavian sailors.

Mountain Monsters

People have told many stories about giant hairy creatures living in the mountains. One of these beasts is supposed to live high in the Himalayas. It is called the abominable snowman or the yeti, which means "magical creature." A similar creature, the sasquatch, is said to live in the mountains and forests of northwestern North America. In the United States this creature is called "Bigfoot."

► **Locate the places on the world map.**

Monsters: Real or Fake?

Activity 2 I Saw...

► Listen to the reports.
► Match each picture with a report.

A Lake Monster

A Mountain Monster

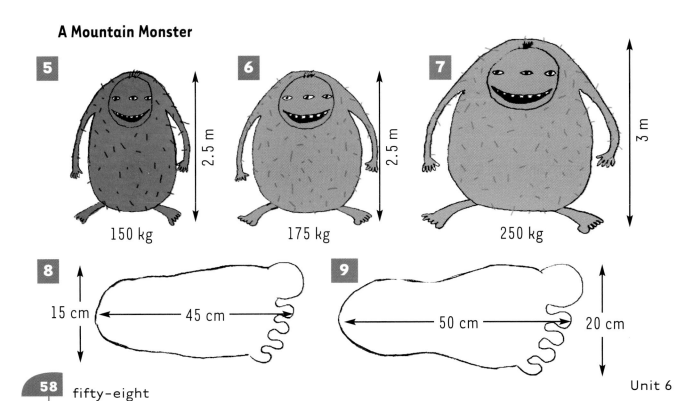

A Sea Monster

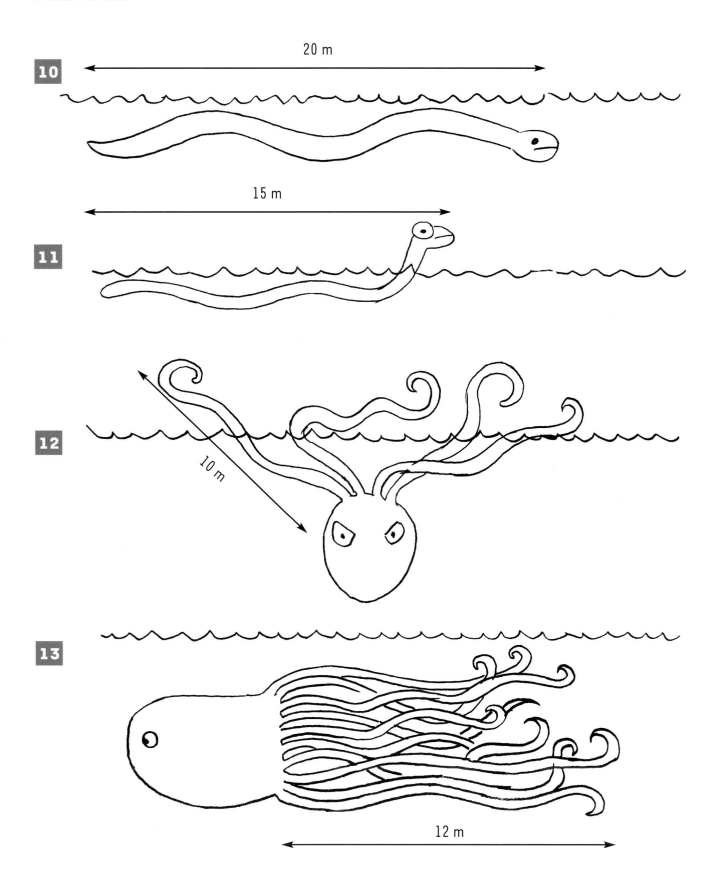

20 m

10

15 m

11

12

10 m

13

12 m

Monsters: Real or Fake?

What Makes a Monster a Monster?

► **Read the texts.**
► **Identify which animals were used to create the monsters.**
► **Identify what makes them scary.**

I'm not really scared. It's only a puppet.

I'm not frightened. I know it's a person wearing a costume.

I feel terrified. These computer-animated monsters look so real.

King Kong

The first real monster movie was released in 1933. It features King Kong, a giant gorilla who is about eight metres tall. He is very strong and aggressive. He destroys part of New York City and terrifies everyone.

Godzilla, King of the Monsters

The movie, *Godzilla, King of the Monsters*, was released in 1956. It was the first of many Godzilla movies to come. Godzilla is a huge lizard. It is 50 metres tall and weighs about 20 tonnes. This monster is very strong. It uses its radioactive breath to terrify the people of Japan.

Ghidrah, the Three-headed Monster

Ghidrah, an enemy of Godzilla, first appeared in 1964. It is an enormous flying reptile. It is 100 metres tall and weighs about 30 tonnes. It has three heads, two tails and a wingspan of 150 metres. It breathes fire to destroy everything that is in its way.

Velociraptors

Velociraptors appeared in the movie *Jurassic Park* in 1993. This movie features many dinosaurs. The enormous velociraptors are the most dangerous. They are approximately four or five metres long and weigh about 300 kilograms. They use their sharp teeth and long claws to attack other dinosaurs and people.

► **Make a list of animals that could become monsters.**

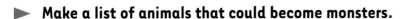

Monsters: Real or Fake?

Activity 4 Monstrous Monsters

Chatterbox 3

► **Look at a sketch of a monster.**
► **Tell your partner about it.**

> It's a sea monster.
> It is ten metres long. It has six long legs. The legs are eight metres long. It has a large round head. It has three big eyes, a big mouth with sharp teeth, and long hair.

> That monster is great! I like it.

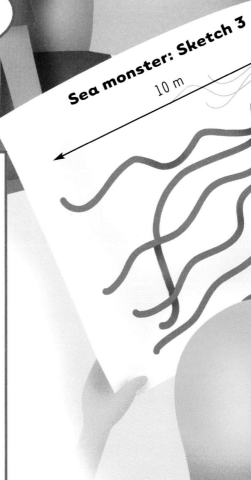

Sea monster: Sketch 3

10 m

Describing Monsters

The monster is big.
It is large/huge/enormous.
It is 5 metres long/tall.
It weighs 20 tonnes.

The monster is dangerous.
It is fierce/ferocious.
It is strong/powerful.

Some monsters have unusual body parts.
One has three heads.

Some monsters have special powers.
One has radioactive breath.

Wrap-up

Create your own movie monster.

▶ **Present your monster.**

▶ **Complete a fact card about the monster.**

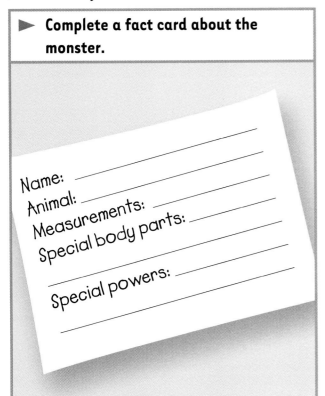

Name: _____
Animal: _____
Measurements: _____
Special body parts: _____
Special powers: _____

▶ **Write a text about the monster.**

Riodan lives in the Atlantic Ocean. She is twelve metres long. She has ten long legs.

the place where the monster lives

a complete description

▶ **Draw a sketch of the monster.**

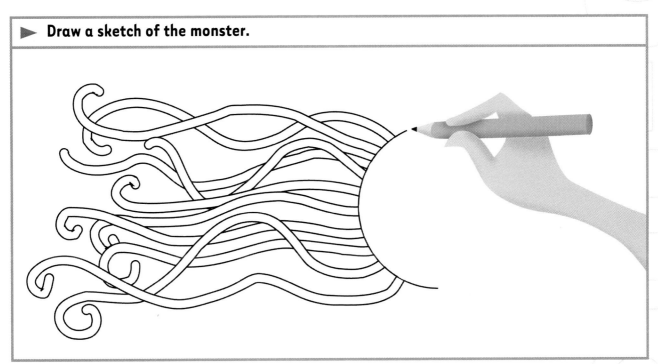

Word Box

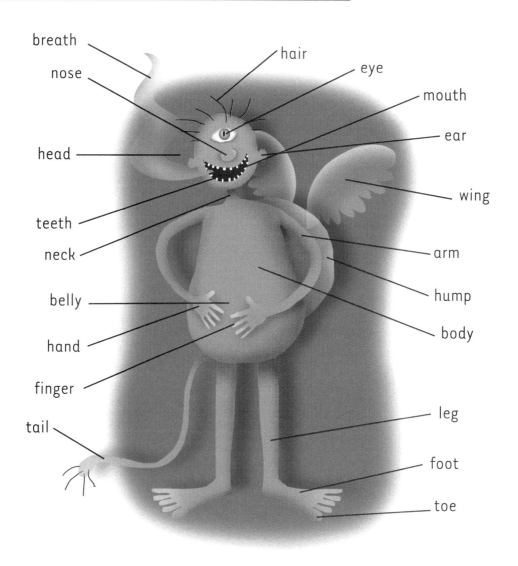

- breath
- hair
- nose
- eye
- mouth
- head
- ear
- wing
- teeth
- arm
- neck
- hump
- belly
- body
- hand
- finger
- tail
- leg
- foot
- toe

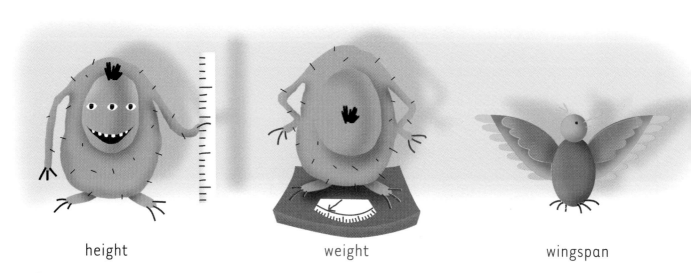

height

weight

wingspan

Tall Tales

► **Can you name any of these people?**
► **Do you know any tall tales?**

 **Tell a tall tale.**

Warm-up

▶ **Look at the book cover.**

Tall Tales
Volume I

The Story
of
Finn McCool

▶ **Find out about tall tales.**

Activity 1 Who's Who?

▶ **Read about the giants of Knockmany Hill.**

A long time ago, in the land of shamrocks and leprechauns, there lived a giant named Finn McCool. Finn was a gentle giant. He loved his family and worked hard for them. His wife, Oonagh, was a happy woman. She was also very, very intelligent.

Where is Giant Cucullin?

Finn and Oonagh lived high up on Knockmany Hill so that Finn could always keep watch for his enemy, Cucullin.

I, Cucullin, defeated all the giants in this country. Now I will defeat Finn McCool.

What's the matter?

Cucullin is coming to challenge me. I am afraid and I don't know what to do.

When do you think he will come?

Tomorrow afternoon. What will I do?

Just believe in me.

▶ **With your partner, make a list of problems that people can have.**

► **Read the next part of the story.**

Oonagh visited all the houses on Knockmany Hill. She borrowed twenty frying pans. She baked twenty-one loaves of bread. She put a frying pan in all but one of the loaves.

Why are you making curds?

Then Oonagh collected twenty large white stones. She set them down in the kitchen. She took a bowl of sour milk and began to make curds.

Get in!

The next afternoon, at sunset, the house began to shake. So did Finn McCool. Oonagh brought out the baby's bed and told Finn to lie in it. Then she covered him up with blankets.

Oh, hello!

Where is Finn McCool?

A Surprise for Cucullin

Chatterbox 6

▶ **Read the next part of the story.**

"Sir, Finn is not here. He has gone to find a giant named Cucullin."

"I am Cucullin and I am looking for Finn."

Cucullin did not know what Finn looked like. He had never seen him. Oonagh stayed calm and talked with the terrifying giant.

It was very windy, so Oonagh asked Cucullin to turn the house around, the way Finn always did. Now everybody knew that Cucullin's strength was in the middle finger of his right hand. He cracked his middle finger three times, lifted the house up and turned it around.

"Have some of the bread I make for Finn and our baby."

Then Oonagh invited Cucullin into the house to wait for Finn. She gave Cucullin one of the loaves with the frying pan baked in it. Cucullin took one bite and two of his teeth fell out. He was not very happy.

"If Finn McCool's baby can eat this bread, he must be a very strong man."

Cucullin took another bite of bread and two more teeth fell out. Finn asked for some bread. Oonagh took the loaf that had no frying pan in it and brought it to Finn. Finn ate the whole thing. Cucullin was amazed.

▶ **Predict the ending of the story.**

Tall Tales

A Real Hero

▶ **Read the ending of the story.**

Oonagh gave Cucullin a large white stone. Cucullin squeezed and squeezed and squeezed but nothing came out.

Cucullin was amazed at the baby's strength. He was surprised and scared.

Finn squeezed Cucullin's hand as hard as he could. Cucullin was impressed. Cucullin put the middle finger of his right hand into the baby's mouth. Finn bit down as hard as he could. When Cucullin took his hand out, he couldn't move his finger. All his power and strength were gone.

Cucullin ran out of the house and down the hill. He was never seen again. Finn McCool jumped out of the bed and danced with joy. His clever wife had defeated the giant.

Tell a tall tale.

► Invent a hero for your tall tale.

► Write a description of your hero.

► Choose a problem for your hero to solve.

► Complete the story.

► Tell the tall tale to your team.

Word Box

leprechaun

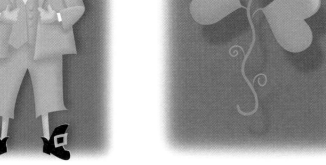

shamrock

thunderbolt

DEFINITIONS

clever: intelligent

curds: pieces of very soft white cheese made from sour milk

sour milk: old milk that is almost solid

tall tale: an exaggerated story

GRAMMAR SECTION

Adjectives

big	bigger than	the biggest
tall	taller than	the tallest
strong	stronger than	the strongest
powerful	more powerful than	the most powerful
courageous	more courageous than	the most courageous

Cucullin was **the strongest** giant in the country.

Oonagh was **more intelligent than** Finn.

The Case
of the Stolen Guitar

▶ Who uses these kinds of tools in their work?
▶ What crime happened?

 **Solve a crime.**

Warm-up

▶ **Read a text about popular-fiction detectives.**
▶ **Identify the detectives and their qualities.**

People of all ages enjoy reading detective stories. People like detectives because they work hard to fight criminals and solve crimes.

A very popular detective is Sherlock Holmes. His sharp sense of observation and logic help him solve crimes others can't. He often works with his friend Dr Watson.

Younger detectives can entertain teenagers. An all-time favourite is Nancy Drew, an 18-year-old amateur detective. Her courage and willingness to take risks help her catch many criminals.

Detective stories appear in books, on TV and in movies. There's such a wide variety that it's easy to find a detective you like.

▶ **Who is your favourite detective? Why?**
▶ **Find some classmates who like the same detective as you.**

Activity 1

The Art of Being a Detective

▶ Listen to a detective. He will describe how he works.

▶ Place the illustrations in order.

Activity 2 The Stolen Guitar

▶ Read the police report about a theft from Newtown Art Centre.
▶ Identify the important information.

Newtown Police Investigation Report

Date Saturday, July 16th, 9:30 a.m.

Facts Jimmy Dee's bass guitar disappeared. It was last seen in his dressing room in Newtown Art Centre, Friday evening at 6:30 p.m.

Description of the guitar: The guitar is red and has four strings. The brand name is "Jupiter" and the serial number is XZT-3658.

Background information: Jimmy Dee is the bass guitarist of a rock group called "The Shiny Stars." In the rock group there's also: Kioko (singer), Nicky (guitarist), Ayiana (drummer), Brandon (singer). The rock group was visiting Newtown for a concert to be held Saturday evening.

What happened? = event	**What?** = object
Who? = person	**Where?** = place
When? = time	**Why?** = reason

▶ **Read the technician's report about the scene of the crime.**
▶ **Identify the important information.**

Newtown Police Investigation Report

Clues from the Scene of the Crime

Facts

Dressing room: no break-in.

Fingerprints: on the door knob of the dressing room.

1 2 3 4 5

Footprints: outside, below the large window next to the entrance. Running shoes, size 9.

Activity 3 — What Do You Know?

► Listen to the interviews of two important witnesses.
► Find more clues.

Telling time

seven o'clock

seven fifteen

seven thirty

seven forty-five

▶ **Read the texts.**
▶ **Identify the eight suspects and their occupations.**

1

Jimmy Dee
  Bass guitarist in the rock
  group "The Shiny Stars."
  He wants insurance money
  to buy a better guitar.

2

Kioko
  Singer in the rock group "The
  Shiny Stars." She's jealous of
  Jimmy's success.

3

Nicky
  Guitarist in the rock group
  "The Shiny Stars." He wants to
  have a bass guitar.

4

Gerry
  Bass guitarist from another
  rock group. She's very jealous
  of Jimmy Dee's guitar.

The Case of the Stolen Guitar

5

Bob Wilson
   Janitor of Newtown Art Centre.
   He needs some money to buy
   a car.

6

Raffaëlla
   Collector of rock-star objects.
   She would like to add Jimmy's
   guitar to her collection.

7

Vladimir
   Seller of high-priced guitars.
   He tries to get excellent guitars
   at good prices.

8

Moira
   Mayor of the city of Newtown.
   She absolutely hates rock
   concerts.

► **Get ready to interview the suspects.**

What did you do on Friday evening? _____	I went to the restaurant.
What time did you have supper? _____	I had supper at six thirty.
When did you leave? _____	I left at 9:15 p.m.
What time did you get back to the hotel? _____	I got back at 9:30 p.m.
Where were you at 7:00 p.m.? _____	I was at the restaurant.
Who was with you? _____	I was with my friends.

Solve a crime.

▶ **Interview each suspect.**

 **?**
 **?**
 **?**
 **?**

 **?**
 **?**
 **?**
 **?**

▶ **Decide who the thief is.**
▶ **Apply for an arrest warrant.**

Newtown Police

Application for an Arrest Warrant

Crime *Theft of a bass guitar*

Suspect

Motive

Evidence

Detectives

The Case of the Stolen Guitar

Word Box

(to) break

break-in

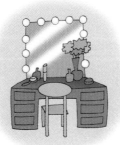
dressing room

footprints

headache

locked

(to) share

stage

unlocked

DEFINITIONS

alone:	by yourself, solitary
a.m.:	in the morning
clue:	something that helps detectives solve a crime like a fingerprint or a footprint
(to) entertain:	to amuse and interest people
p.m.:	in the afternoon or evening
willingness:	a strong desire to do something

GRAMMAR SECTION

Regular past: -ed

arrive / arrived
finish / finished
lock / locked
open / opened

Irregular past:

am / was
break / broke
do / did
drive / drove
go / went
leave / left
steal / stolen

Loonies and Toonies!

► **What is this medal made of?**
► **What are some things that represent your community?**

 **Design a class coin.**

Warm-up

► **Discover some characteristics of money.**

► **Guess which of these objects could be used as money.**

Activity 1 Money Makes the World Go Round

► **Listen to the story of money.**

► **Compare your predictions from the warm-up.**

Loonies and Toonies!

Activity 2 Coins and Culture

Chatterbox 14

► Read the information about your coin.
► Complete the coin card.

► Listen to your partners.
► Write the information on the coin cards.

Activity 3 Let's Remember

► **Read the text.**

Circulation coins are used to buy things but there are other types of coins. Commemorative coins are designed to honour a person, a place or an event.

► **Listen to the interview.**
► **Look at the commemorative coins.**
► **Guess what each of the coins honours.**

Activity 4 Let's Celebrate Our Community

Chatterbox 12

► **Choose symbols that represent where you live.**

Why don't we . . . ?	Do you think we can put . . . ?
How about . . . ?	I'd like to put . . .
What about . . . ?	

Wrap-up

Design a class coin.

► Read about the contest.

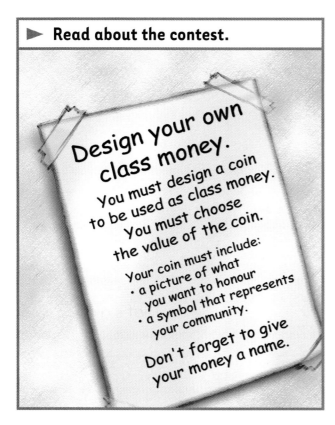

Design your own class money.

You must design a coin to be used as class money. You must choose the value of the coin.

Your coin must include:
• a picture of what you want to honour
• a symbol that represents your community.

Don't forget to give your money a name.

► With your classmates, decide what you will honour on your coin.

- Our province
- Our community
- Our school

► Work with a partner to design your money.

► Tell your classmates about it.

► Vote for the money you like the best.

Loonies and Toonies!

Word Box

beaver

dime

loon

maple leaf

nickel

penny

quarter

raven

schooner

sugaring off

Treasure Hunters

► What kind of chest is this?
► Who do you think it belongs to?

 Play Treasure Hunt.

Warm-up

► **Look at the picture.**

► **Test your knowledge of pirates and their treasure.**

Activity 1

Dirty Jane and the Pirates

▶ **Read the story.**

Dirty Jane was a pirate. She was the captain of a large ship and crew. Dirty Jane and her crew attacked many merchant ships in the Caribbean Sea. They stole gold, jewels, pistols and other valuables from these ships. Every merchant ship was afraid of Dirty Jane and her crew.

One sunny day Dirty Jane and her crew celebrated a great victory. They defeated another merchant ship and took all its valuables. The pirates started to divide the booty. "We have all this treasure because **I** am the **best** pirate captain in the world. I want three-quarters of this booty," announced Dirty Jane. John Longhands quickly responded, "That's not according to our contract." Big Henry, the first mate, took a piece of paper from his pocket. He read the words aloud. "One-half of all the booty goes to the captain, one-quarter goes to the ship's pilot and one-quarter belongs to the crew. It says so right here."

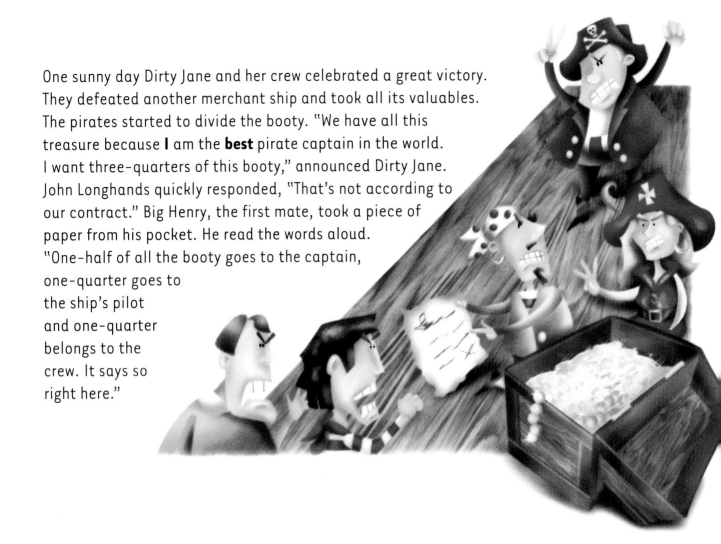

All the pirates were very angry. They thought their captain was unfair. "Dirty Jane is greedy," they said. "Down with the Captain," they yelled. "Make Big Henry our captain," they shouted. They threw Dirty Jane into her cabin and locked the door. She was their prisoner now. "We can sail the ship without her," they boasted.

That night a violent storm hit the ship. The wind became stronger and stronger, and the waves rose higher and higher. "Take down the sails," ordered Big Henry. The wind and the sea battered the ship hour after hour. Suddenly, the ship hit something. An enormous wave broke over the ship, and the ship rolled onto her side. Big Henry and all the pirates panicked.

"Abandon ship!" shouted Big Henry. "Quickly to the boats!" screamed John Longhands. "We're sinking!" cried the pirates. They were so afraid! They forgot Dirty Jane. They forgot the treasure. They jumped into the lifeboats. "Row! Row for your lives!" ordered Big Henry. The pirates rowed away into the dark and stormy night.

Treasure Hunters

The next morning the sea was calm and the sun was shining again. Dirty Jane broke down the cabin door. She went on deck. She saw pieces of lifeboats floating near the ship. "I must be the only one who survived," she thought. "They abandoned ship. We hit a sandbank, that's all. A sandbank means we are near an island. The silly fools!" She collected the booty, some food and a few pistols. She put everything into the last lifeboat. She rowed to the island.

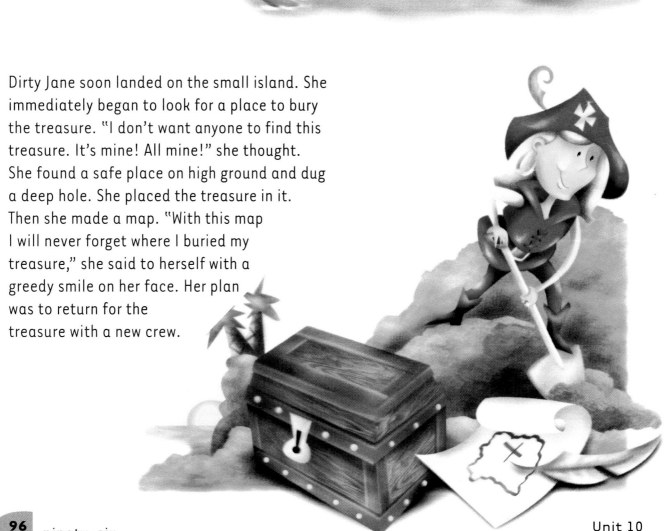

Dirty Jane soon landed on the small island. She immediately began to look for a place to bury the treasure. "I don't want anyone to find this treasure. It's mine! All mine!" she thought. She found a safe place on high ground and dug a deep hole. She placed the treasure in it. Then she made a map. "With this map I will never forget where I buried my treasure," she said to herself with a greedy smile on her face. Her plan was to return for the treasure with a new crew.

For thirty days Dirty Jane stayed on the tiny island. She waited and waited for a rescue ship. One morning a pirate ship landed on the island. Dirty Jane ran to the ship and cried, "Please take me aboard."

Dirty Jane sailed away on the ship. No one knows if she ever returned for her treasure. Imagine, that treasure may still be there . . .

Activity 2 Buried Treasure

► Listen to the directions.
► Find the buried treasure.

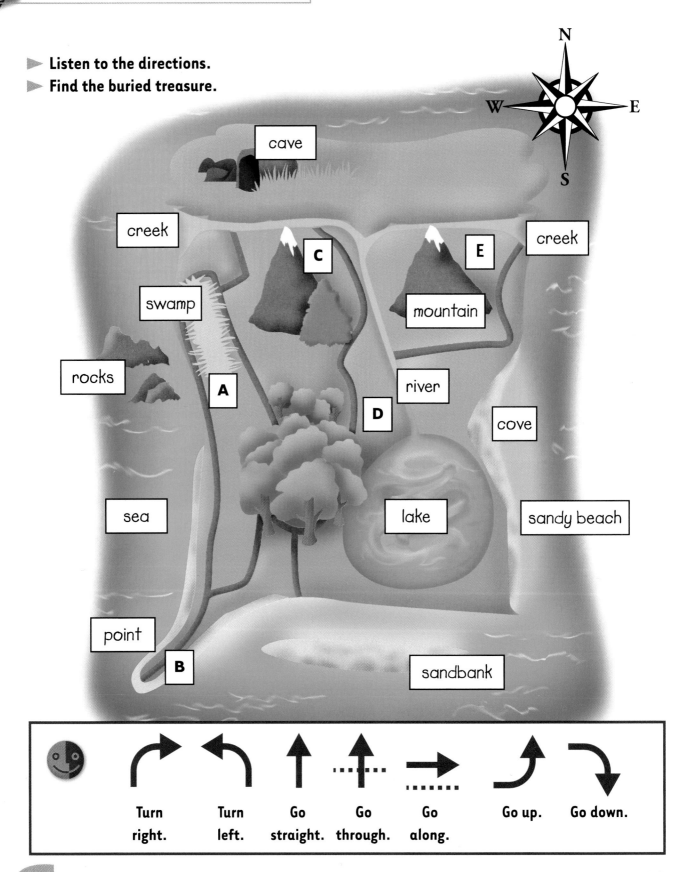

| Turn right. | Turn left. | Go straight. | Go through. | Go along. | Go up. | Go down. |

Activity 3 Find My Treasure

► **Prepare your game board.**

Place a sandbank and rocks on the outside squares.

Place a forest, a lake, a cave, a swamp and a mountain on the inside squares.

Place your treasure on one of the squares.

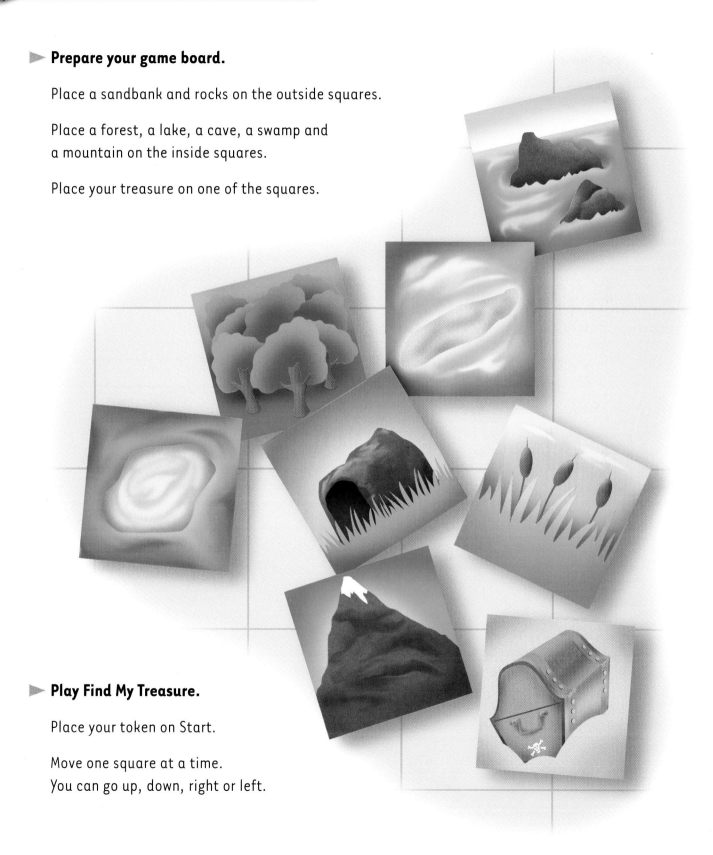

► **Play Find My Treasure.**

Place your token on Start.

Move one square at a time.
You can go up, down, right or left.

Activity 4 — Get Your Gear!

▶ Look at the equipment needed to go on a treasure hunt.

▶ Suggest one use for each object.

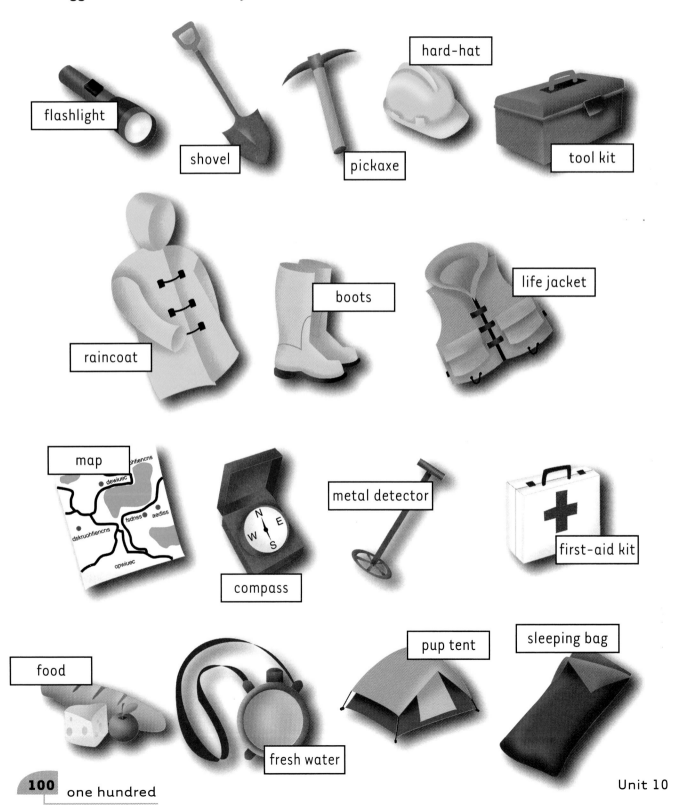

flashlight

shovel

pickaxe

hard-hat

tool kit

raincoat

boots

life jacket

map

compass

metal detector

first-aid kit

food

fresh water

pup tent

sleeping bag

Play Treasure Hunt.

▶ **Write down ten items that you should take on the treasure hunt.**

flashlight
shovel
fresh water

▶ **Write one question about the story.**

Who is . . .

?

▶ **Read the rules and play the game.**
1. Pick a challenge card.
2. Use the proper equipment to face the challenge.
3. If you don't have the equipment, return to Start.

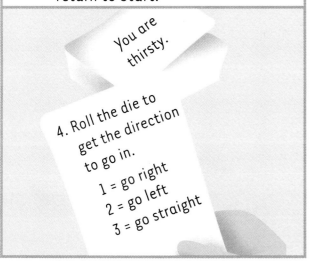

You are thirsty.

4. Roll the die to get the direction to go in.

1 = go right
2 = go left
3 = go straight

▶ **Answer three questions.**
If you don't know the answers, you can't get the treasure.

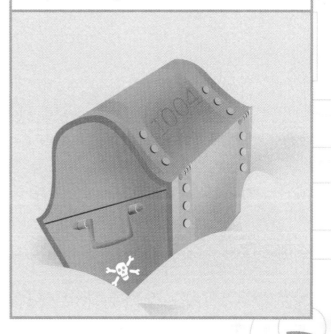

I'm the BEST in the entire universe!

angry   (to) boast   booty   (to) bury

It's all mine!

crew   greedy   jewels   ship

(to) throw

wave

Unit 11

Don't Bug Me!

► **Do insects bug you?**
► **What makes each insect unique?**

 Make an insect guidebook.

Warm-up

▶ **Survey your teammates.**

▶ **Find out which insect is the least popular.**

Activity 1 Don't Let the Bugs Bite!

▶ Name the insects.
▶ Classify them as harmful or not harmful.

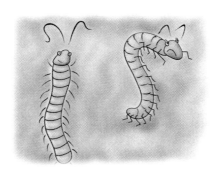

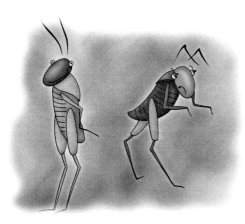

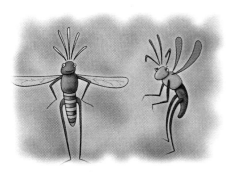

Activity 2 The Bug File

Chatterbox 9

► Read the descriptions.

Insects

There are over a million species of insects in the world. Less than five percent of them are harmful! Read on to find out more about the wonderful world of insects.

Mosquitoes are very small but they can really make you itch! Only the female mosquito can bite. Mosquitoes love water. During the day, they stay in a cool, dark place but when the sun goes down, they come out to eat! Mosquitoes can be dangerous because they can spread diseases such as malaria and yellow fever. They also transmit the West Nile virus. These are very serious diseases.

Ants are tiny but they are very, very strong. Some can carry up to fifty times their own weight. Ants eat small insects, nectar and honeydew. Ants are very social insects. They live in large colonies. Sometimes there are 100 000 ants in one colony! Each ant colony has one queen and many workers. Most of the workers are females. Ants are like humans because they live like a big family. The workers take care of the babies by feeding them and washing them. Ants can even communicate with each other. They tell each other where the food is and they warn each other of danger.

Where there is food, there are flies! Flies are the most common insects that bug us! Flies are seen mostly in the spring and summer when the weather is warm. Flies move very quickly. They sense movement and react five times faster than humans. That's why it's always so difficult to swat them. Flies aren't very scary but they can be harmful. They are always around garbage and rotten food. Then they land on the food that we eat. They can carry bacteria from one place to another.

Many people are afraid of bees because they can give a nasty sting. Only the female bees sting and they can sting only once. When a bee loses its stinger, it dies. Bees are good for the environment because they help fruit and vegetables grow. They fly around to collect nectar and pollen. Bees live in colonies where there is one queen and many workers. Some nests have up to 80 000 workers. Bees look after their babies in their nests.

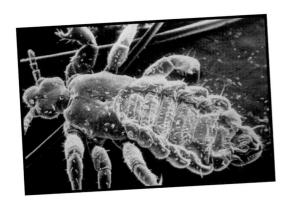

Fleas are so tiny you can't see them but you can certainly feel one bite. Fleas jump around from person to person to get blood. They live in hair and clothing. Fleas contributed to one of the greatest disasters in history. In the 14th century, they spread a disease called the Black Plague throughout Europe. Watch out for these little pests.

Crickets are the singers of the insect world. The male crickets sing to attract females. Crickets can be heard from spring to fall. They are only a few centimetres long but their song can be heard from far away. Crickets can be found in fields and even in your backyard. Some farmers don't like them because crickets like to eat young plants.

Cockroaches slip through cracks in the walls and run across the floor. They hide during the day but come out at night to find food. Cockroaches will eat anything. They love dark, damp places. Cockroaches usually live in old buildings and houses. They are found in dirty places but they are not dangerous at all.

The funny thing about centipedes is that they don't all have one hundred legs! They can have between 30 and 340. Imagine if they had to wear shoes! Centipedes live in dead leaves and trees and are sometimes found in basements. Their front legs are actually poisonous fangs. They use them to catch other insects. Don't touch them. They can bite humans too.

▶ **Compare your answers from activity 1.**

Activity 3 Get a Job!

▶ **Read the job ads.**

Nurses needed. Must be able to take blood very quickly. Must be tested for infectious diseases such as malaria and yellow fever.

Can you move quickly? Are you ready to work at night? Can you climb walls and squeeze into small, dark places? Become a SPY!

Wanted: Construction workers. Must be very strong. Must be able to carry 50 times own weight. Must be a good team worker.

Farm workers needed to work in the fields to collect pollen and nectar. Must be able to work with others.

Athletes wanted for track-and-field team. High jumpers needed.

Singers needed for outdoor concerts. Must be ready to work during the summer.

Salesclerk needed for shoe store. Must be comfortable working with feet.

Garbage collector: Must be able to move quickly. Should not be bothered by dirt.

Activity 4 — What Did You Call Me?

▶ Find the insect to complete each idiom.

> 😊 Idiom: a phrase or expression that has a special meaning
>
> I'm warm and cozy. I'm as snug as a bug in a rug.

He works all the time.
He is as busy as a _____ .

She is always moving.
She has _____ in her pants.

He's a very gentle person.
He wouldn't hurt a _____ .

▶ Invent your own idiom.

Wrap-up

Make an insect guidebook.

▶ Choose an insect.
▶ Complete the insect description card.
▶ Draw a picture of the insect.
▶ Place your ID card in the class insect guidebook.

Name: centipede

Habitat: dead leaves, trees, basements

Characteristics:

Our Class Insect Guidebook

Word Box

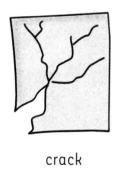

crack

fangs

harmful

(to) itch

snug

(to) sting

(to) swat

tiny

Unit 12

Up, Up and Away!

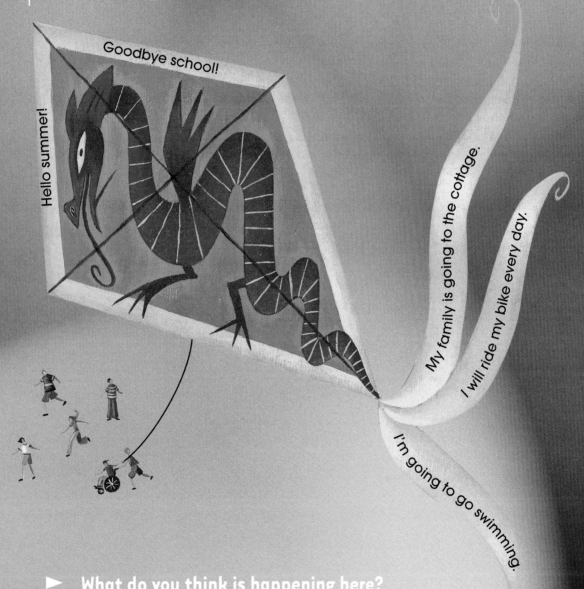

Goodbye school!

Hello summer!

My family is going to the cottage.

I will ride my bike every day.

I'm going to go swimming.

► **What do you think is happening here?**
► **Do you have a kite?**

 **Design a kite.**

Warm-up

▶ **Look at the different kites.**
▶ **Describe the kites.**

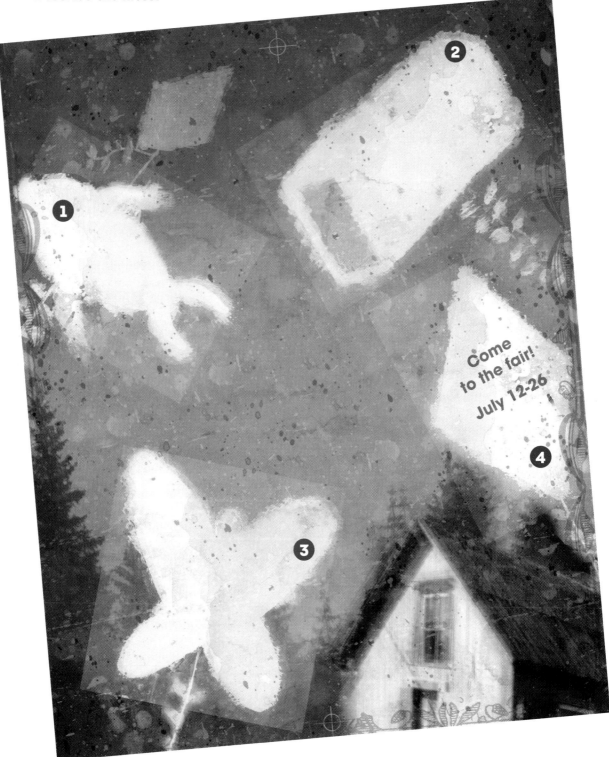

Come to the fair!
July 12-26

A String of Kites

► Listen to a boy and girl talking.
► Explain what their kites are for.

Up, Up and Away!

Activity 2 Paper Magic

▶ **Read the texts.**
▶ **Choose a kite to make.**

File Edit View Special Help   10:34

Kite News

Students fly kites with messages to their parents.

http://www.home-madekites/~kiteconstruction/

Materials you will need:
- paper
- paint or markers
- string
- scrap paper for the tail

http://www./home-madekites/~kitestyle1.html

Carp Kite

Fold a large piece of paper in two.
Draw and cut out a fish shape.
Decorate the fish.
Write messages on small pieces of scrap paper.
Glue the messages onto the kite.

http://www./home-madekites/~kitestyle2.html

Traditional Kite

Take a sheet of regular paper.
Draw and cut out a diamond shape.
Glue straws to form a T across the kite.
Decorate the kite.
Write some messages on the kite tail.

Activity 3 Gone with the Wind

► Read the messages.
► Write your own summer messages.

I want to swim every day.

I am going to music camp.

My brother and I are going to visit our aunt in New York.

I will play baseball with my cousin.

My family is going camping.

Up, Up and Away!

Activity 4 Poetry in Motion

▶ **Read the poem.**
▶ **Write your own summer poem.**

Summer's here!

No more schoolbooks,

No more rules,

Just bikes and baseball

And swimming in pools.

Wrap-up

Design a kite.

▶ **Decide on the model you want to make.**

▶ **Design your kite.**

▶ **Write some messages on the kite tail.**

▶ **Write your poem on the kite.**

Word Box

butterfly

cottage

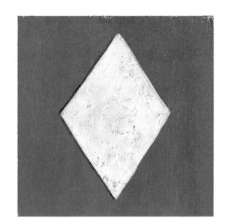

diamond

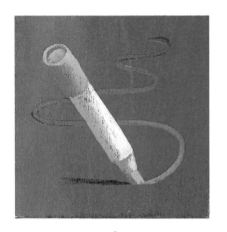

marker

scrap paper

straw

string

tail

(to) tie

Reader's Theatre

Let's write a short play and read it to the class.

1. **Plan your play.**
   - Choose a story.

A fable

A well-known story

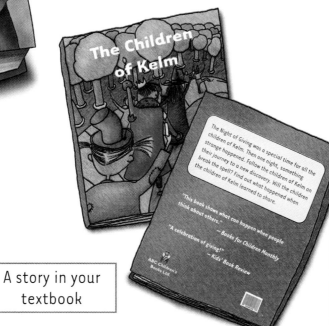

A story in your textbook

- Read the story.
- Identify the characters.

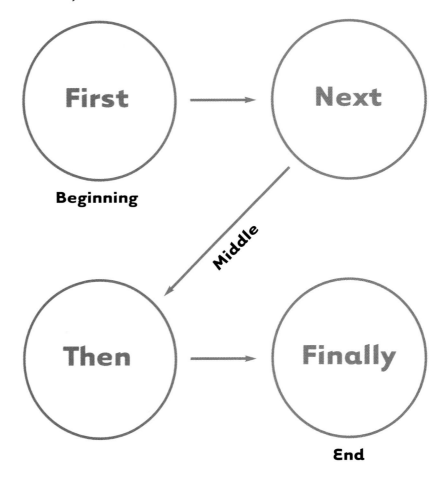

CHARACTERS
Muron
Shan
El
A stranger
Other children
Muron's mother
An old woman

- Write the storyline.

First
Beginning

→

Next

Middle

Then

→

Finally
End

2. Write your script.

- Use one or two narrators to tell the story.
- Use the characters to act out the story.
- Write the characters' lines.
- Finish your play.

NARRATOR 1: The children had to go to the village to find their parents but they were frightened. Muron had a plan.

MURON: We will go on the Night of Giving. People are kind then.

ALL THE CHILDREN: That's a fantastic idea!

PROJECT 1

3. Rehearse your play.

You're On!

Think about a person you admire and tell your classmates about this person.

1. Decide how you will work and who you will present.

a comic book hero

a character from a story

an athlete

a television star

a movie star

a musician

a friend

a family member

Other:
_____
(Check with your teacher first.)

2. Decide how you will present the information.

I will:

- write and perform a monologue ☐
- videotape or tape-record an interview with the person ☐
- role-play an interview with a partner ☐
- write a biographical text about the person. ☐

If you have other ideas, make sure to check with your teacher first.

3. Think about where you can find information about this person.

in books

in encyclopedias

in magazines

on CD-ROMs

on the Internet

4. Find the information.

5. Prepare your presentation.

Here are some ideas for different types of presentations:

Monologue: Prepare a text presenting information about yourself as the character. (Remember to use the first person. For example: "My name is . . . I have appeared in over 45 movies.")

Interview: Prepare interview questions to ask the person you will interview.

Role-play interview: Prepare a series of interview questions and answers with your partner.

Biographical text: Prepare a text presenting information about the person. (Remember to use the third person. For example: "She was born in Argentina." "He was a hero to many people in China.")

Chatterboxes

Chatterbox 1   Asking for more time

Are you ready?

Just a minute, please.

- ▶ Wait a minute.
- ▶ I'm not ready.
- ▶ Hold on.
- ▶ Can you wait, please?
- ▶ Just a minute, please.

Chatterbox 2   Asking for help

Can you give me a hand, please?

- ▶ Can you help me, please?
- ▶ I need some help.
- ▶ Please help me.
- ▶ Could you please help me?
- ▶ Can you give me a hand, please?

Chatterbox 3 Asking for clarification

► Sorry, I don't understand.

► Can you repeat that, please?

► How do you say . . . in English?

► What do you mean?

► What does this mean?

Chatterbox 4 Working and playing with others

► It's your turn.

► It's my turn.

► Roll the die.

► Pick a card.

► Give me the die, please.

► You're next.

► Whose turn is it?

► Time's up!

Chatterbox 5 — Inviting and suggesting

- Do you want to work with me?
- Do you want to be my partner?
- Let's do the work.
- Let's work together.
- Why don't we . . . ?
- How about . . . ?
- What about . . . ?

Chatterbox 6 — Agreeing and disagreeing

- I agree.
- I think so.
- I disagree.
- I don't think so.
- What do you think?
- That's fine with me.

Chatterbox 7 — Encouraging others

- That's great!
- Well done.
- That's a good idea.
- You're a good partner.
- Good for you!
- Congratulations!

Chatterbox 8 Talking about work

- Have you finished?
- What did you write?
- I wrote . . .
- Is this O.K.?
- Is our work all right?
- How's this?
- Do you think this is all right?

Chatterbox 9 Dividing the work

- Who will do this?
- I'll do it.
- What do you want to do?
- I want to . . .
- What would you like to do?
- You can be the . . .
- Let me . . .

Chatterbox 10   Starting an activity

- Let's begin.
- Who will go first?
- I'll start.
- What should we do first?
- I'm first.
- You go first.

Chatterbox 11   Encouraging others to speak English

- Let's speak English.
- Say it in English, please.
- Please speak English.
- Remember to speak English.
- Remember, we have to speak English.

Chatterbox 12   Working quietly

- It's too noisy.
- Be quiet, please.
- Sh! Not so loud.
- Can you please speak quietly?
- Let's be quiet, O.K.?

Chatterbox 13 Asking permission

- May I . . . ?
- Can I please . . . ?
- Could I please . . . ?

Chatterbox 14 Offering help

- Can I help you?
- Do you want me to help?
- Do you need help?

Chatterbox 15 Warning others

- Careful!
- Look out!
- Watch it!
- Stop!